*"Sex is just a word.
What matters is the connection the word implies."*

- tonii

MOIST
AN EROTIC ANTHOLOGY

iiPUBLISHING

MOIST An Erotic Anthology
© 2020 Copyright of individual pieces remains with the contributors.

First published 2020

Copyright notice
All rights reserved. No part of this book may be reproduced in any form or by any electronic or mechanical means, including information storage and retrieval systems, without permission in writing from the authors or publisher.

Published by ii Publishing in conjunction with Poetix University

Cover design: tonii
Design and layout: Nupur Nair

Edited by Ahja Fox and Dara Kalima

ISBN: 978-1-7362167-0-5

Printed in the United States of America

ii PUBLISHING
New York, NY
www.toniiinc.com

Welcome to literature made for pleasure.

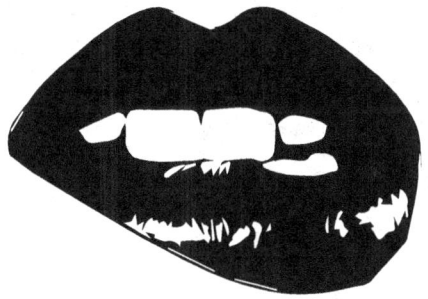

A message from Our President

This anthology is different from most books you will ever read. It is raw, liberating, and explicit, and yet it still provides an experience that honors the art of poetry. I have found no other topic as liberating for both the poet and their audience as erotic poetry. In this genre, sex is brought out of the shadows to provide an experience that has the power to change perspectives, start conversations, and introduce concepts that might not have been experienced "behind closed doors."

The words that will follow are brought to you by a group of talented poets, who attended the Poetix University's writing workshop called MOIST. In this three-day workshop, students were prompted to express some of their desires, sexual experiences, and their most passion-filled and intimate fantasies. The students were instructed to share their feelings and thoughts without filters, concerns, or restraints. This has resulted in a collection of poems with words that are not only read but can be felt as you progress from page to page.

We are here to showcase this collection and the poets in the same way we promote other poetic material because sex is just a word; what really matters is the connection the word implies. Our hope is this book will allow sex to come out from "behind closed doors" and encourage people to discuss, express, and discover the sexier sides of themselves.

So, I ask for you to allow this book to whet your desires, fantasies, and predilections while stimulating feelings and thoughts within you. These words, if permitted, will free you to view sexuality, intimacy, and attraction in a new way.

Now, let us take you there.

tonii
President of Poetix University

"Let our lips strip within each other's grips
As our tongues entangle in a tango
Leaving our minds to step into ecstasy."

"I need you to listen closely as I approach your ear."

I want to
write a poem
that has you
dangling
at the very tip
of my tongue
holding on to my taste buds
for dear life or
from extreme pleasure
as I tell you all
the juicy things
I will do to you or
that we will go through.
I want to lick
all the crevices of your brain so well that
you'd think it was your privacy
that my tongue was fondling
but that is for later,
right now,
now
just listen to my words
and let them
subtly
run up and down your skin
as if
they were a feather, or
my fingertips, or
my nails,
whichever is your pleasure.
Your pleasure
will be mine, too.
Just focus in and feel
my deliciously sensational
sensation-filled words
caress and graze over your skin
informing you of how finely divine

you are to me,
words helping you feel like
your most sexiest self
because in this moment
you are just that.
...
How is that feeling?
Are you
with me?
...
I hope so, because
I need you to listen closely
as I approach your ear
with my amorous laced verbiage
delivering promises
of what is to come.
Reverberating
moans
nibbling softly
on your yummy earlobes...
Do you feel that?
The stimulating sensation
of my tongue
circling that canal
as my breathy whispers
sends anticipatory chills
coursing up your back?
Should I also
run my fingers up and down
your spine?
...
Will that make you
feel
fine?
...
Do you like that?
...
I hope you do because
in being this verbally close to you
I can't help but notice
your devilish grin and

the eagerness of your inhales
as your body anticipates
our next sin.
Ohhh...
how much I love
how my words feel
against your caramel skin.
And my vocabulary,
it so enjoys that taste of
your salty sweetness.
Can you taste mine?
...
Are you mine?
....
Are you
still with me?
Because I want each
syllable that I next
ex-press to
se-duc-tive-ly
kiss
your
neck
with
each
and
ev-
ery
noun
pro-noun
ad-jec-tive
and verb
especially
the verbs
leaving subtle
traces of my lipstick,
as my lips
stick and linger
with that last word
leaving a fresh flushed hickey
so that you remember me,

always
in this moment.
...
Are you feeling it?
...
Yeah,
you are feeling it...
...
My dear,
this is only the beginning,
and the way your heart is racing,
your veins are pulsating
and your breathing keeps changing
and the way you are now sitting
erect at the edge of your seat
back at full attention,
let's me know
you are ready
for all the things my
tongue and lips
can and will
do to you
but
this poem
was only ever going to be
verbal tease
that had you dangling
at my every word.
But since I aim to please,
let's take this elsewhere
to create the rest
of this masterpiece.

"Desire in Poem Form"
Zoetic Fyre

"I want the taste of your skin to awaken my manhood."

I trust you to lead me tonight,
Let all my senses take over,
Touch you, taste you, smell you, hear you,
Simply put I'll enjoy you.

I'll totally let go,
Allow myself to get caught up,
In our own shared experiences,
Show me a brand new world.

I want to touch your body only using fingertips,
I have no doubt that I can map it out,
I want the taste of your skin to awaken my manhood,
Causing me to throb with longing to take you.

The sound of your breathing while blindfolded,
Leaves me in the dark filling with anticipation,
Going down on me and my heart pulsating,
Feeling the anticipation, wondering what happens
    next.

Then making me taste your sweet tender juices,
Oh baby, I cannot refuse it,
Licking you and licking you until your legs quiver,
Then when you ask me to fuck you, I come hither.

Stroking you deeper and deeper 'til the climax,
It was liberating that's a fact,
Oh, it was such a great fuck,
Blindfolded sex liberating in the dark.

"Blindfolded Sex"
DP

"...spanks me so hard, I start to scream and cream all over his knee,"

Welcome to my dark, twisted world of fantasy,
Where I don't have one, but multiple realities.
But for the purpose of this session,
I will tell you this desire,
And it's how I wish to be a submissive wearing a collar.
In my mind, my Master calls me a petulant little bitch,
As he slaps my wrists in cuffs,
Preparing his whip.
But before he whips my cheeks,
He spreads me across his lap,
And spanks me so hard, I start to scream and cream all over his knee,
Which angers him even more to my pleasure you see.
Because I made such a mess,

He rips my blouse,
Exposes my breasts and flushed red chest.
He pulls my nipples with his fingers,
And twists them until I moan.
I feel another orgasm beginning to grow.
But before I could climax,
He sticks his member in my throbbing mouth,
And I suck and suck while he pulls on my collar.
"Enough of this" he says and pulls out.

And begins to plunge me from the rear,
While dripping hot candle wax on my back.
"Do you like it when I ravage you?
Do you like being my Slave?
Do you like it when I fuck all of the good out of you
    to give you pain"?
And I say, "Yes, Master, I want to be your dirty slut
    forever.
Thank you for fulfilling one of my dark and twisted
    fantasies."

"Dark and Twisted"
The Black Rose

"Measure every inch of my dick With the length of your tongue"

Please
...
Please me
By placing your lips
Around the perimeter
Of my phallus
With talent and skills
Make me feel
Every sensation
Secreting semen
Throughout this session's duration
Oral satisfaction
Creates a reaction to my mid-appendage

Approach cautiously
But patiently
Pay attention to him rise
Inside the confines
Of your mouth

Allow your tongue to rotate
Around my shaft
To graft pleasure
With suckage
Being rhythmically applied
While you slide with strides of pressure
In your up and down motions

Measure every inch of my dick
With the length of your tongue
And glisten with spit
As you let it
Slither until gag
Reflex lags until reaching tonsil depths
As you hold it there until none is left
You have learned how to hold your breath

Besiege me
With gliding and stroking
Guiding me down open
Throat choking on my erection
Blowing like smoke
Dick soaked and coated
Salivated affection
A concoction of saliva and semen

Sustain your slow pace
Show me your face
Filled sufficiently
With my pickle in your jaws
Jack my shaft simultaneously
My breathing erratic
Then you build me up to a pause
...
I cease
I shake
I melt
...
Magic made
With the persistence perfected
In the pleasure you caused
I popped
And painted your oral walls
Like Warhol
Filled you with my graffiti
But tenderly yet savagely
...
You swallow it all.

"Warhol"
tonii

"Moan in satisfaction as you perform your witchcraft."

Pull me in close, lightly kissing my neck.
Slowly guide your nails from the back of my head to my chest.
Allow your fingers to be a paintbrush, my body your sketch.
Ask me if it feels good, and I'll simply say "Yes."
Slightly moan in my ear, while you rub on your breast.
Put your hands in my pants, feel me sluggishly getting erect.
Nibble on my ear, I welcome the slight pain.
I am now rock hard, we can now begin the game.
Remove my pants and push me on the bed.
Handcuff my hands over my head.
Kiss every area around my dick, make me squirm as you tease me.
Rub your lip on my tip, make me beg for you to please me.
Look up at me, as your tongue flickers down my shaft.
Moan in satisfaction as you perform your witchcraft.
Seize my balls, squeeze and release.

Force deep breaths to replace my speech.
Place the head in your mouth... Ohhh Shit it's so warm.
As the saliva fills your mouth, it's like a natural chloroform.
Clasp my dick with both hands, devour it to its base.
Slow and strategic is how you win this race.
Let it slide down your throat, as your esophagus constricts.
Close your eyes and inhale, yes, breathe in this dick.
Exhale it out your mouth while giving your tongue a twirl.
Now is the time you make my toes curl.
Bob up and down, each time increasing the suction.
Keeping your eyes on me is how you appease the seduction.
Gradually get faster as my body begins to take flight.
As I concentrate to contain the eruption with all my might.
You feel me pulsating, my body is losing control.
"FUCK!!" is all I can say as you snatch my soul.
You give me a wink because you know you've reached your goal.
Your confidence is so sexy, I begin to explode.
As I burst, you open your throat to receive my load.
This is only round one, round two, we switch roles.

"Round One"
The Gentlemen from San Francisco

"use anything for our pleasure, and my orgasmic torture."

Since, we are locked inside,
I decided to shop
around the house.
I'm glad to have found
some strawberries and
whip cream,
now, how about dessert
being on me?
And I know bandanas
are now for outside use but
today, in here
don't cover my mouth,
you'll want to hear the purrs
from my lips,
you'll not want
to muffle my sounds,
but do blind my eyes instead,
and, as to not leave marks,
I grabbed the saran wrap.
Wrap my wrists
to this here headboard or
bind them together
either way, tonight,
I am your
love toy,
here solely for joy,
play with me
how you see fit
until you opt to fit in me. But
before either of us peak,
I just want to give you some permissions,
I affirmatively consent
to us being up to no good,

all for our greater good
so at this moment you could
use anything for our pleasure,
and my orgasmic torture.
Treat me roughly and
tease me gently,
I'm trusting you implicitly to
get me to cream, and
eventually make me scream
but how we get there,
is up to you.
You've got everything
in this house as your tools;
ice, belts, forks, even soft fabrics,
as long as you supply that
engorged magic.
Call me what you want,
make me say what you wish,
every part of me
from toes
to
tongue
including my words
are part of this deal,
let's make this a moment
one we'll look back on and
still, feel.
So here I lay,
ready,
for your use,
use me in every way.
You are the master,
to me the bound and
blinded sex slave,
slay
away.

"Saran Wrap and Bandanas"
Zoetic Fyre

Between thighs I crave
Consuming your elixir
That pink strawberry

"Haiki #1"
The Gentlemen from San Francisco

"...tease them with the tip of your tongue, or all of it, I don't really care."

Don't look at me there, it's dirty
No seriously this can't be
What do you mean returning the favor?
That's not what my culture taught me
No, it's not rose petals
Don't call it that while your fingers send shivers
As they trace my skin
No, you're not supposed to see this, it's filthy
But how am I supposed to say no
When your breath burns my inner thighs?
Pearl size sweat on my forehead, bedsheet in my fists
I can't help but squeal when you taste me
Is this how it feels to be kissed on my core?
Feels like bliss and torture rolled into one?
I feel your lips move on my layers and I don't have to
    open my eyes to know how I wanted to erase
    that smug smile from your face
Well what are you waiting for? I said, the impatience
    blinded me followed by regret

As your tongue comes back to take all of me
More, I said
Please, right over there
Deeper, I said
Please, can you touch me deeper?
My body, my soul, want you to spread the petals
And take it all
Oh yes, tease them with the tip of your tongue, or all
  of it, I don't really care
All that I know is that I want your tongue and then
  some more
Take me, all of me, and don't stop
Let your fingers dance furiously and take me to the
  top
Please, is it wrong to want more?
Would you want me to spread it like this or like that?
Don't laugh, how am I supposed to know that oral
  could go both ways?
If I knew this kind of pleasure beforehand
I'd ride your head off into the sunset

"Cave's Sweet Torture"
Agni Locke

"grip my jaw, pry open my wet lips, and thrust your tool in..."

The curtains are pulled back,
I feel only the moonlight teasing my skin,
I know I'd said I wanted you to
take me to a place I'd never been,
but here I am, slipping into an orchestrated darkness,
ready to dive into your world
of the seen and the unseen.
A cloud engulfing my eyes,
my breath trembling in my throat,
I feel you lightly grind your shaft in
my butt crack,
and a terse hand fondling my tits,
calling me your prize.
My heart is pounding as you scoop
me up without a warning note;
Pray, what jungle are we heading to,
leaving our warm and predictable
love nest?
As you lay my lithe bare body
on a foam mattress
(my arms instinctively reaching out
to feel the bed frame),
I can only guess
I was in for trouble.
Maybe the right kind?
A voice goes off in my head.
"You're my bitch tonight.
Just do as I say and
you'll come out of this alive," you growl.
There, there,
this looks nothing like a joyride.
Anticipation building up inside,
I trust your judgment
as you slide
one finger then two,
making me suck on them

for dear life.
Next, your mouth grabbed mine
with the force of a
starving man,
seeking his pleasure for every dime.
My tongue entangled in yours,
I've got no choice.
You choke me with your urgency,
and I concede, I've clearly
lost my voice.

Beneath the darkness of the silk scarf,
I absorb the scent of your cologne,
your damp body pulsating
against my own...
this doesn't seem half as bad,
I relax, thinking to myself.
But you pull the rug from under my feet
as you rise over my body,
grip my jaw, pry open my wet lips,
and thrust your tool in,
telling me to savour the whole length of it, right 'til
    the tip.
Am I shocked or tantalized?
I sure can't tell.
I obey
as you fill my mouth with your
cream,
you keep going harder,
I choke;
There's apprehension in every pore of my body,
I want to plunge in deeper,
but also scream.

"Do you feel debased enough,"
you ask
as you relieve me of the weight
of your dick,
now, rubbing it between my breasts,
pinching my nipples,
slapping my ass.

I groan,
my pussy inflamed with desire
and my juices trickling down
to the sides of my thighs.
If this is how a journey to Nirvana feels,
maybe I'll lie back and experience it all
without using my eyes.

"Take me already," I moan.
You lick me behind the ear,
making me melt into
the safety of your earth,
then swiftly,
You push your sneaky little
middle finger into the vortex
of my womanhood.
Making me cry out in surprise,
then writhe in ecstasy,
"Baby, we're just getting started,"
you say it loud and clear.
As you slide down a little
and
hold my boobs, sucking on them
like you are drawing life
from their softness and hardness.
Mmmmmm...
You murmur,
rubbing your chin against my nipples,
circling the areola with your tongue.
I shiver,
my back arching, pushing
my breasts deeper in your mouth.

Then just like that,
You slide further down,
this time going for the deep dive.

You rub my clit,
play on the side of its pinkness,
occasionally teasing me
by making me lick the wetness
clinging on it.
My breaths come in rapid,
my whole body rising up
in sacred submission.
But hold on,
a minute goes by,
and then a few more,
I reach out to feel your hair
under me,
but only feel a suspicious air,
hanging over this sultry night.

My heart thunders,
naked, helpless, and out in the open
(with probably a pervert neighbour
spying in),
I'm like bait to a sea of sharks.
Where did you go, Mark?
I perspire,
on the verge of regretting
the extent of my insatiable desires.
Just when I ready myself
to quit this game,
you swoop in,
caress my cheeks and tell me
to act like an obedient dame.

"Turn around," you say
"Get on all fours,
and let me take you to a place
you have never been."

I comply,
offer my ass, and chuckle, "you're my boy"
dig into the comfort of the mattress,
eager to be your lover, whore, and mistress.
Your hardness tears through
the pulp that is my vagina,
You yank my hair like a brute,
grab my tits.
We're not done yet, you
mock me, slowing down,
and before I can comprehend
the source of a strange new sound,
I feel another pair of rough hands

rubbing my cheek,
teasing my lusty lips,
and taking them apart to
make me suck on a lubed tip.
Sliding in, and then sliding out.

"What the..." I gasp, ready to fall
into a stupor,
"But baby, this is your birthday gift,"
Mark whispered in my ear.
Tonight's your night,
have all you can and more.

"A Birthday Gift"
IRF

"Stick your tongue deep in my crevices..."

Can you do me a favor?
Yes.
Can you eat out my pussy?
Could you lay shoulders square
At the base of my chalice
And drink gulps.
Lick the dregs of the source;
From every curve of the Gates
That keep it moist...
Can you keep them wide open?
Push the flesh back like a curtain.
To reveal the only magic show you'll need to see:
Me gushing;
Perfuming your mustache
That's tickling, teasing my clit.
Can your lips replace it?
Kiss my clit like a newfound lover
Make out with her like you love her,
More than me,
While still satisfying us 3.
Tell   me   your ABCs
While pushing up my knees
To reach my shoulders.
Get bolder.
Hover over my pussy platter
Before you take your meal:
A ravenous soldier
On the front lines of my needs.
Can you go slower?
Move back down,
Sliding your hands,
The length of thighs,
Moving from the outer meat
To the dark meat,

Massage it.
Get those juices ready for your second helping,
Provided,
You rotate your head to infinity
To bring me beyond
Child's play;
This is where adults live.
Satiating sensual appetites,
Stick your tongue deep in my crevices,
Let my legs squish your head as you drill in me
Fill me with your intention to taste heaven,
Moan so I know how good I taste!
Can you grab me tighter?
I want your nails to leave imprints,
My canal to mold around your dick print;
You pressed in so deep.
I want your savagery.
Show me how well you can use me
For your own needs,
Growl as you sully me,
Make me forget words
While I twist and contort under your cravings!
Can you kiss me
Like it will be our last
While holding me like there's no past
Present
Future
Suture?
The wounds left from wanting
When my body was against me
And I felt deserted in this life
Remind me what it's like breathing;
As my inhale is your exhale
Rubbing thighs with closed eyes,
Memorizing how we feel in each other's arms.
Can we do this again tomorrow?

"Questions"
nora oz

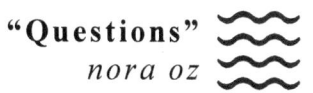

"As my face was buried into a feminine's pubic shell."

"Happy Birthday Darling" read the card attached to
    the flowers on my desk.
Continuing on, it expressed: "Today is your special
    day, and as such, I want you to meet me in the
    woods by the lake."
Without haste, and in anticipation of this surprise,
I met my lover following the closing of the sun's eyes.
He was waiting for me and had quite a spread,
And with a smile on his face, he placed food on my
    plate.
After I ate to my heart's desire, he opened up a box
    with a smirk that grew wider.
"I have one more surprise" he whispered in my ear...
"but I need you to turn around and relinquish all of
    your cares. Will you obey, my Dear?"
Before I could answer,
Satin fabric was placed over my eye,
And I was thrown into darkness
With my fate splattered on his ravenous plate.
He squeezed my breasts from behind
As the anticipation caused me to gush
And led me with both hands to a place that felt like
    strong wood.
He leaned me against the sturdy pillar which felt like
    a tree
And proceeded to bound me with more fabric so I
    could not flee.
"I want the moon and stars to see how wicked I can
    be. Tonight, you are all mine, and not even this
    tree could save you with the depths of me."
As he finished talking, he French-kissed my neck and
    then took his tongue to lick the other side
    making me even more moist and wet.
His deep kisses and luscious licks turned into bites
    all over my face, ears, and lips.
He traced my mouth

And then stuck his finger into my hole and told me to lick not one, not two, but three of his fingers (his middle, his pinkie, and his thumb).
But lo and behold, there was another set of hands removing my clothes—the energy felt feminine as there was a softness in tone.
This second set of hands raked their nails down my chest to my breasts and landed on my stomach to blow on my navel's rest.
What felt like branches spreading my legs apart,
My panties were torn
To expose my vulnerable parts.
One finger entered me
And I let out a cry
While my familiar masculine rubbed his fully erect penis on my left and right side.
I was told to bend over and stay
While what smelled like chocolate slid into my perineum to taste.
More chocolate and also strawberries I began to smell
As my face was buried into a feminine's pubic shell.
So as chocolate was being licked from my crack,
And I was forced to eat strawberries out of the feminine's Garden of Eden,
Leaves were also caressed on my back to tease me in ceding.
As he finally throttled me from behind,
I began to scream,
The echoes in the forest reverberated back to me.
"Do you like your birthday gifts?"
"Do you like your fucking presents?"
When I did not answer, the feminine pulled my tits with one hand, and with the other, slapped my behind until I finally climaxed all over his throbbing prick.
When I finally came down from all of this, I whispered into the air: "Thank you Darling for my birthday surprise. May I have many, many, more Solar Awakenings."

"Happy Birthday Darling"
The Black Rose

"It's all good
As long as you cum."

Hey ladies.
Let me tell ya about last night.
It was so intense and rough.
We lasted the whole night and morning,
took a nap and then went back to it.

> But what exactly did y'all do
> when doing the deed?
> Girl, you know these are the details
> I'm gonna need.
> Was there long foreplay or
> did y'all just play for hours?
> Did it feel heavenly or were y'all up to some shit
> that required immediate showers?
> Are you going to tell us the tale?
> What. are. the. details???

> Did he hit it from the back
> did he hit it from the side,
> did he let the tongue slide
> on your lips,
> tease your nips,
> turn on the nectar faucet
> with a flick of his wrist?
> You know we need a little warm up before the games
> begin
> and the best kind is when you leave your fragrance on
> his chin.

Actually, I don't need the details,
keep that between the two of y'all,
but do tell me this little bit of information.
What's your favorite position?
Doggy, missionary, reverse cowgirl?
Lazy dog, spooning, wheelbarrow,
And then there's oral and anal?
So, what are your thoughts?
Which best ensures your pleasure?

For me specifically,
I like them all, but if I had to choose,
I'll take the top.
The rodeo position.
The bull-riding-soul snatching-sit all on it,
      Missionary Style.
It's something about this position.
You know it's about to be good when the dick first
      enters
And I sit down fully on it.
This position right here gives me all control.
The control where I can look deep in your eyes and
      into your soul,
and at the same time, tighten my walls around your
      shaft.
And there I am.
Grinding on you slowly while rubbing on your arms
      as you grab my waist,
moving it in the same motion for deeper penetration.
Hitting the top of my walls while my eyes roll to the
      back of my head.

Now, let me bounce up and down,
inhale, exhale,
walls tighten and release.
You then wrap your arms around my legs and begin
    pounding me some more.
And just when you think you're in control,
I move my legs into that squat position
and now that ass is taking over.
You take part in lifting me up
and right before I explode,
you lift me to your face
sucking my juices at a rapid pace.

                Hmm,
              Interesting...
                Okay...

                                I hear you...
                  ...but you ever have it from the side,
                    when the angle matches the curve
                      so you get the whole girth,
          hand on your stomach so you can't escape,
nipples enveloped in lips so you won't want to?
                Now he's stimulating your clit,
            Two fingers rubbing lightly in a circle
                    while still stroking.
Eyes look into yours, daring you not to moan,
                        pumping real slow
        Until his hips raise and his hand shifts.
           Body hovers above so you can
         watch every strike hit its mark.
           Feel every strike hit its mark.
                That sensual spectation
            makes mental stimulation,

leading to sexual satiation
with a new rush
of your yearning,
now he's gliding in and out even faster,
riding the wave of your want
and then up goes one leg,
leverage,
so his hand can grab your ankle,
bring the leg farther than you thought you could
stretch
and the thrust brings a tear to your eye because
nothing should ever feel this good.
Melt into goo
as you cum for the second time.

I disagree but umm okay...

I hear you both.
I now know that you
are team leg up and
you get off on riding steeds but
back shots is where it is at,
on your knees or standing up,
satisfaction is guaranteed.
Tall or short, much girth or
on the skinny side,
this position is
the great
equalizer.
See, riding only works with a medium size,
too big and you can't sit,
the less blessed,

you can't feel at all and
you might not even connect,
and being on your side is
hit or miss, hitting or missing
your spot while the poker's pointing
in wrong ways but
some pounding from the back?
I am here for all of that.
Dicks hit walls with all
of their force and
with a tuft of my hair in their hand,
I'll arch my back with
my eyes
rolling the same.
Even a mediocre lover
can make this work and
an exquisite lover?
...mmm...
I'm shaking just thinking of the
quaking his member can

make me do… so yeah,
you can keep your leg in the sky game or
your giddy up pony
bucking and grinding—
Backshot Daddy can
tattoo his name
on my pussy's membrane.

    You know, you may be on to something

Na, I'm going to stick to my position

    Hey, have it your way!
    But you know what

It's all good

        As long as you cum

"Memoir of Our Labias"
LP'2020, nora oz, & Zoetic Fyre

"Her licking her clit and then her licking her clit..."

Something I had always coveted,
A threesome with a light-skinned and dark-skinned
      chick,
Both curvy with phat asses,
It happened in 2015, it was fantastic.

All three of us getting naked,
The time had come, I finally made it,
Both me and the dark-skinned lady sucking on the
      light-skinned chick's tits,
Then her doing the same thing to her, next would be
      the clit.

Her licking her clit and then her licking her clit,
Both working their way up to my dick,
Both taking turns going down my shaft,
Working their way up to the best sex I ever had.

First, it was the dark-skinned chick,
I stuck it in her tight slit,
With every thrust exciting her and hearing her moan,
While the light skinned lady gets turned on recording
      it on her phone.

Then the dark-skinned lady wanted to watch me bang
      the light-skinned chick,
And then it became her turn to receive the dick,
I hit her from the back, she was so delighted,
Making the dark-skinned chick so excited.

The dark-skinned chick said fuck her harder,
I want to hear her moan louder and louder,
Fuck her like you never fucked a woman before,
I want to hear her moan more and more.

It got more exciting, I did not want to stop,
Then she wanted to ride me, she came out on top,
Missionary, forward and reverse,
It was so hot; I was getting ready to burst.

Then the dark-skinned lady wanted another turn,
I went back to her and began banging her,
Hitting her doggy style and almost giving her a
    charley horse,
But we were so into it she did not care that she felt
    sore.

She kept wanting me to fuck her harder and deeper,
The light-skinned chick was kissing her,
It was my fantasy finally coming true,
This kind of threesome, I always wanted to do.

Then I climaxed but I came inside the condom,
I would have liked to have come anywhere on them,
Ass, tits, mouth,
But my fantasy was finally realized, that's what
    counts.

"The Threesome I Always Coveted"
DP

"The warmness of her hotbox was like when Heaven meets Hell."

As the steam from the shower dissipates, a voice cuts through the mist from the bedroom. "Baby, come here."
My body still dampened with water; I approach the room only to be greeted by a single chair.
"Baby, sit down."
Unsure of what is going on, but I find clarity in the familiar sound.
I oblige... promptly met with a surprise of kisses on the back of my neck and caresses on my thighs.
She whispers in my ear, "I'm sorry," as she binds my hands behind me with one of my silk ties.
She can tell I am perplexed.
Borderline vexed.
Because we both know these ties cost too much to be playing with sex.
But that gets overshadowed by what comes next.
She places a blindfold over my eyes, and asks, "Do you trust me?"
"Woman, I'm sitting here butt naked, soaking wet, tied to this chair and that's the question you ask me?"

She hits me in the head and says, "boy you're silly?"
Then proceeds to saunter off quickly.

They say when you lose one sense all the others heighten.
So I know I heard her leave but the mass of the room didn't lighten.
Something brushed against me, it had a nice sweet smell.
It was a foreign presence, but enticing as hell.
The being began to straddle me, I was taken aback.
Because I knew this wasn't my baby with an ass like that.
She began to grind on me, I felt her pussy glide.
It was an intoxicating rhythm, then she put me inside.
The warmness of her hotbox was like when Heaven meets Hell.
She started riding me and I began to yell.
I felt her pussy grabbing my dick, each stroke magnified.
I was lost in her sauce, she had me mesmerized.
I was ready to foreclose on that pussy, grab my luggage and reside.
Then the familiar voice came in and said, "It's my turn to ride."

She hopped on, but it wasn't like how it felt before.
She came for a battle, aiming for a high score.
The last pussy was wet, but this tsunami drenched my sword.
She jousted for supremacy while moaning, "Give me more."
I felt my legs get weak; knees buckled in the chair.
As she thrust her pelvis into me while gripping my hair.
Then she began to slow down, I can hear her creaming on my dick.
Hands began to touch me all over, thought it was a magic trick.
The unknown being began moaning and licking on my ear.
As she began to unbind my hands and guide me out the chair.

Led me to the bed where I laid on my back.
Then straddled my face and offered a delectable snack.
I consumed her nectar as if it was the ultimate life source.

My tongue was driving her to heaven, her moans
    assured it was the right course.
Suddenly, a warm moistness engulfed my shaft.
My body jerked from the surprise, but immediately
    soothed from the bath.

Not being able to see, made the ecstasy escalate.
I could feel my climax approaching and I was ready
    to accept the fate.
I was still devouring her passion fruit as she reached
    heaven's gate.
She arrived, when I arrived, made me ejaculate.

The room went quiet and then the door closed.
She dismounted my face and removed my blindfold.
I scanned the room for some kind of evidence.
Hoping to reveal the identity of the occupant.
But my Lady's smile was all I saw.
She had just surprised me with a ménage trois.

"Surprise"
The Gentlemen from San Francisco

"This blindfold
Is the costume specifically designed
For my inner freak"

He came home and told me let's try something new
Took off his tie I think it was blue
With white stripes
Slightly oversized on one side for style
Then began to not so gently place it over my eyes
When I winced he tied tighter
So I quickly learn not to complain
Knowing from past experiences with my lover
That our greatest pleasures usually started
With a little pain
He disappeared for just a moment
But it felt like forever
Seeing that I can't see
Each second felt like an infinity
But then he touched me
And I felt my temperature surge
I knew then that tonight my sexual energy I'd purge
I just hoped that I had the courage to trust him
Him who has blindfolded me not knowing
That this blindfold
Has turned me from princess to villain
So all of these thoughts
He had of me
Being tender and sweet
I tell him to put a pin in it
Because tonight we're fucking
Since you've blindfolded me
I can't see
Myself
Being bad that is
So unknowingly
You've placed this blindfold on me
Not knowing that

This blindfold
Is the costume specifically designed
For my inner freak
He kissed me roughly
I grabbed him rougher
Standing up to bend down so that I can suck the cock
    of my lover
Making my way around the shaft and balls that I
    began to orally rediscover
Since I'm blindfolded, I can't see that I have gotten
    spit all over his thighs and the covers
I'm so focused on gargling one ball while I massage
    the other
I felt his body start to tense and I knew it was time
    for the next phase to commence
I laid him down
Mounted him like a stallion no saddle
Arched my back then let him in
Sheathing his dick with vaginal juices
Bouncing so hard my blindfold begins to loosen
I tell him to hold it, he grabbed the blindfold and
    my hair
My back arched and my pussy spit
My vagina is thumping hard on his dick
I scream I'm about to cum and he says me too
I said wait let me show what this blindfold makes
    me do
I dropped back down to my knees
I sucked my cum off his dick
I mean I sucked that shit clean
I made him cum
In the back of my throat
All the way where my tonsils hang
He simply looked at me when he finished and said
Oh yeah, we gotta do this again
This whole blindfold thang

"Blindfolded"
Meka J. Woods

"Reach, embrace, and feel me"

Beauty holding gaze
Look closely. Much to behold
But don't touch just yet.

Inhale aromas
Intimacy is the smell
Whet your appetite.

Reach, embrace, and feel
Soft, moist, delicate and yours
Fondle how you will.

Tasty flavored treat
Pineapples and cherries sweet
Eat up the yummy.

Don't stop but listen
Purrs, sighs, moans, screeches, and screams
Deep breaths. Ahh sated.

"Love in Five Haikus"
Zoetic Fyre

"Did I tell you I know how to ride a wave or two?"

You've had your eye on me
since we met last month at Cafe Brew,
now that we're alone in my living room,
take off that mask of propriety,
let me see through you.
I know your hands wanna go all
over my tits, and your cock
in my mouth,
Boy, I'll let you have them for supper,
once you taste my clit
and pleasure me down south.
Start by peeling the denim
off my lush, toned thighs,
plant a hundred wet kisses on the underside,
prepare well to move up and enjoy the real prize.
No, no, don't dive in yet...
Play with my lady underthing, tease me wild,
let your fingers do the talking (oh, I meant the
    rubbing),
make it a hungry, torturous ride.
If you couldn't tell, my pussy's catching
fire now,
so tell me what that mouth can do,
colliding on bare skin, and how!

Start slow, lightly touching the outside
of my swollen lips,
slide a finger (or two) in my cunt,
as your hands tug at my perky nips.
My back against the closet, one
trembly thigh over your shoulder, I moan,
tell me, how does it feel eating me standing up, like a
    speck of
nasty in your monochrome?
Come on, part those, throbbing lips
with your untamed tongue,
flick it slow, flick it fast,
or penetrate to drink from my
juiced up walls,
I don't care, no matter how you love
me down there,
you can't go wrong.

Fuck! Oh, my fuckin' God! The way
your lips meet mine,
I'm building up a tremor inside,
I'm losing my mind.
No wait! Stop! I can't take it,
the way your fingers and your tongue
explore my darkness,
but holy fuck! I WANT IT!
This bittersweet agony,
is that how it felt when I flashed you
some at the Sunday meet-and-greet?

I'm the lady here, you're the man
so scoop me up in your brawny arms,
toss me on the couch or the bed,
push my buttons, turn on
every damn switch,
whisper dirty in my ear,
say you want me,
that you'll stroke and pet me,
before you part my legs,
bring out of shame my wicked secret,
and treat me like I am
your greedy little bitch.
Suck me soft, suck me hard,
let me grab your hair,
and see you breathe hot and rough,
pleasing my lady parts.
Call me names, both sweet and scandalous,
interspersed with love and lust,
but don't shrink away when I call you some,
we are our own light in this lonesome
dark tunnel,
why shy away then, from dredging up
our wolfish selves and coming undone?

Did I tell you I know how to ride
a wave or two?
If you will submit, I can ride your face too...
So lie down, and reach up baby, tear off my frilly top,
unhook my bra, suck on my breasts,
admire the sweat beads on my
voluptuous mound,
as I grip on the sides of the crumpled bed sheet,
leaning in to let you have your fill.
Don't forget, we're just starting,
because I want you to devour me whole
in a second round.

"Slurp Fest"
IRF

"Open me and lick..."

Tease my cocoa skin,
With your flickering wild tongue,
Navigate my body.

Open me and lick,
Like Carvel and Dairy Queen,
Taste my sweet ice-cream.

Smell the endorphins,
Secreted in the moist air,
Sweat, musk, and perfume.

Hear my cries and sighs,
Moans, expletives, grunts, and yells,
Listen to my Soul.

Third Eye staring me down,
As it pierces beyond flesh,
Your gaze transcends sex.

"Haikus of Stimulation"
The Black Rose

"...I couldn't tell which was wetter, the rain or me"

Tonight was long overdue
I've been craving him for way too long
I nearly drooled when he walked through the room
His eyes were met by candlelight and lingerie
I intended it to be yet another night he won't forget
By the look on his face, he had the same idea in mind
Wasting no time, his tongue wrapped around mine
And I couldn't tell which was wetter, the rain or me
He kissed and bit my neck and tore me out of my bra set
Then proceeded to play with my clit as he licked and sucked on my breast
He knew exactly how to make me melt in a matter of seconds
I brought his eyes up to meet mine and told him, *"lay down"*
Once he was comfortable, I stretched my leg across his face and hovered over his head
He slid his hands around my waist as I proceeded to lower my hips and fuck his face

My honey dripped on his lips as he sucked on my clit
and my head fell back
Mouth opened wide I let out a loud moan of relief
It must have been music to his ears because he began
french kissing my clit and sticking his tongue
in the canal of my sweet water river
As I ooh and ahh with my eyes closed tight, I gripped
the back of his head and whined my hips as my
juices covered his face
The licking and slurping sounds escaping his mouth
made my mind run wild
I let out a laugh and bit my bottom lip
He slaps my ass and grips it, confirming that he
knows the dragon in me has been unleashed
"That's right, just like that"
My breathing slowed down into a trance, the dragon
has taken over
My whine began to quicken and my demands became
louder
Body trembling, I melted into a puddle on top of him
A night he won't forget turned into a night we both
will remember

"A Night to Remember"
L. Rose

"Let's fuck each other until we explode like the fireworks in Montreal..."

Wake me up going down on me,
It's as beautiful as a sunrise in Greece,
And let me go down on your bush,
Like the Garden Of The Gods in Italy so lush.

Let's have wet and wild sex in a Jacuzzi,
In a hot tub, I'm freaky, sue me,
In the Poconos, we can move to the bed with rose
      petals,
Ride me like a motorcycle, put the pedal to the metal.

So wet and moist like soft rains in Punta Cana,
Me, like the mountains in Adirondack, so hard,
Let's fuck each other until we explode like the
 fireworks in Montreal,
Let's turn each other inside out.

Now we're asleep on a beautiful sunset in North
 Carolina,
But that doesn't mean times up,
We'll do it tomorrow, again; I'll be your
 monument in DC,
I'll once again ride that wet pussy.

"Wake Me Up"
DP

"Your robe just opens
So I peek the erection"

Your showered body
Drips pussy wetting perfume
Make me melt for you

Teeth biting my ass
As I walk past to make tea
Thus the games begin

Your robe just opens
So I peek the erection
Rising to claim me

Your mouth tastes like me
Intoxicating peach musk
And ice cream divine

My favorite sound
Your moaning growl in my ear
Cuming from behind

"Sighkus"
nora oz

"Insert your tongue for the sweetest part of my fruit."

And so it begins,
The part where we have to leave our 50 Shades of
    Grey themed room.
The part where we return to our normal daily non-sex
    lives.
The part where we can't get out of the bed and off of
    each other.
The part where your arm is wrapped around me
    feeling on my booty,
And I'm laying on your chest,
Stroking your shaft.
And so, it begins,
We hit snooze a couple of times because we don't
    want to leave this moment.
You kiss my forehead then make your way to my lips.
We stare at each other and I already know what time
    it is.
You kiss my neck and caress my breasts.
Your mouth slowly and romantically moves down my
    body.
You have quite an appetite and I've served up a juicy
    meal.

You kiss those lips gently, letting me know you're
	about to get started.
Use your tongue baby and lick me up and down.
Spread my legs with your arms.
Use your fingers to open me up.
Insert your tongue for the sweetest part of my fruit.
Move your tongue in circular motions.
Open your eyes and watch me go crazy.
Open your mouth wider and begin to eat.
Suck a little harder now and feel my release.
As you suck the last drop come up for air;
Tell me you love this pussy,
And dive back for more.
Nibble on my piercing and stick your fingers inside;
Insert two then add more.
Lick roughly in circular motions.
Feel my legs shake crazy and hear my moans echo on
	the walls.
I'm cumming, baby, I'm cumming.
You suck the last drips out,
And as your eye connects with mine, my soul is now
	forever yours.

"More"
LP'2020

"Let's skip the forbidden tree and go straight to planting your seed."

Splitting my legs as you kiss up my thighs,
I would tell you where to lick,
but you read my mind.

Charismatically,
You fall in sync with me.

Touch on my butt and move your tongue.
Find the rhythm while you flick my clit.

Satisfy as you settle between my thighs.
And make my moisture seep into the sheets.

Bring me to that point and then relax.
Send me into an addiction that makes me love the
    relapse.

Give me tongue that makes me cum.
And makes my God Spot pound like a drum.

And when you're all done,
Flip me over and have your own fun.

You see,
The way you listen makes me crazy.
Like you have tapped into the feminine energy and
    choose to nurture me.
You treat me in these moments as if I am your Eve.
Let's skip the forbidden tree and go straight to
    planting your seed.

Move through me,
I want to hear your noises.
I want to cum simply from your enjoyment.
Finally, I can hear you,
On the brink like you can't handle.

Move with me and let it all go.
I want to feel you unload.
And when you're done,
Tell me that you love the sounds that I make
    when I cum.

"The God Spot"
B.S.

She commands the room
Sashaying as she exits
Her fragrance lingers

"Haiku #2"
The Gentleman from San Francisco

"Feeling that pussy wet like a swimming pool..."

In my house, all alone,
You're not home,
You're 1,000 miles away,
Getting hard thinking about you all day.

Longing for your touch,
I want your sex very much,
Come home so I can rip those clothes off,
Throw you in the back and fuck.

You had a long bus ride, well rested,
I know you want the dick, I sense your message.
Already wet, you rode in a Greyhound,
Now hop on a ride with me; it's going down.

Stroking deeper and deeper like I hadn't fucked you
    in a long time,
No music but still we fuck and grind,
Feeling that pussy wet like a swimming pool,
As with every stroke, louder moans coming from you.

Then after we climax, you ask for seconds,
But we just finished, I hadn't been ready yet,
But you're still wet, longing for more dick,
Telling me to put it back in and quick.

We fuck and fuck 'til we both climax,
Explosive like gunfire in Wyandanch,
We finally did it, like the first time, it was great,
Your pussy was worth the wait.

"In My House"
DP

"...it deserves the flick of his tongue and the touch of his hand..."

When I hear his steps outside my door, I lie down on my bed,
Open my legs and think of England, Lady Hillingdon said.
They said it was found in her journal in 1912,
Although if you were to tell me that so and so aunt told their niece this last week, I won't bat an eye.
I was told and taught that sex is a duty, an obligation we should bear
That when we are unwilling, we still have to do it because our partners want it.
I always thought that my vagina had no capability to reject,
That it means to always take in what is erect.
But not again,

Never again will I lie on my back and think of
  England.
Why should I when the boy with the golden smile,
Could always brighten my day with a little trip
  downtown?
Why would I think about England
When his sweet mouth and skillful fingers make me
  hotter than the Sahara?
I will not let them make me just lay down and think
  of England again,
For my vagina to be silenced again.
For it deserves the flick of his tongue and the touch
  of his hand;
My vagina has a voice and it deserves to be heard.
So if St. George is what she wants then St. George is
  where I go,
I'll ride the boy with the golden smile 'til there's no
  tomorrow.

"I Will Not Think Of England"
Agni Locke

"I am a jar filled with olives,

And his task is to pit me and consume

my flesh."

Sultry kisses under cherry blossoms in Tokyo rain,
Udon noodles slurped from around my neck,
As a distant peak of Mount Fuji sits picturesque,
    placid, and peacefully in the Southwest.
Moving from Japan to South America, my partner
    takes me on an exploration of his Brazilian
    nuts,
And I give him a taste of my two coconuts.
We run wild in the Amazon,
And bathe naked in the falls,
Before moving to Greece where we become each
    other's Mediterranean detour.
I am a jar filled with olives,

And his task is to pit me and consume my flesh.
He is my Spanakopita, filling and rich,
But we soon travel to Italy where my vagina becomes his cannoli.
Our final destination lies South of the equator as we hike through Kenya parched and thirsty.
To quench this thirst, more wet kisses arise,
As we both exploded on the Elephant Hill Hiking Trail.
Capturing some shots of Nairobi, and exploring the Bombas at night, we engaged each other in stories of Kenyatta's last fight.
Pleasure, passion, and stimulation galore,
I'm so happy to have a passport.
What more could any woman ever ask for?

"Passport"
The Black Rose

"Watch out here comes the dressing, extra cream"

I want you to toss my salad
Make sure you don't forget a thing because I like my
    veggies
I'll provide my own dressing
If you provide the rhythmic chopping
Then we can get this shit popping
Now I'm going to name the ingredients
Real slow
I want you to repeat after me
Say lettuce
Three
Times
Slow

Then add just a bit of carrots
Like you're making a slaw
Now get ready to roll your R's
To give me a little Rrradishes, Rrraisins and Rrruby Rrred tomatoes
Whoa nelly if you double up on those veggies that'll be sure to make the dressing flow
But wait you can't forget the protein so
Legume
Legume
Legume
LEGUME LEGUME ME
Now finish it off with some cheese please
UH OH
Watch out here comes the dressing, extra cream

"Salad Bar"
Meka J. Woods

"I slurp what you squirt

And clean up what you secrete

secretly"

My tongue
Moist, soft, and salivating
Tenderly touching your clitoris
And covering it with
Heat, lubrication, and stimulating sensation
With each stroke, rotation, and pressure applied
Combined with my lips
Working inside of your dips
I surround every fold and crease
While my tongue slips in between
I sip on your pussy like coffee with sugar and cream
Suckage sounds increases your sensitivity

As I increase the intensity and frequency
I slurp what you squirt
And clean up what you secrete secretly
My mouth, chin, and cheeks are slippery
Lubricated by the lubrication you leak naturally
Your back bows, curled toes, hands steering my head
      where you want me to be
Devouring rhythmically
Shivering trembling, convulsions
Sporadic euphoric motions
From me delivering ecstasy orally
With the diction in my tongue
You now lay limp, insensitive, and numb
From mere words in a poem
Perfectly orated in the creation of your cum.

"Orate"
tonii

"suck on my clit until my soul has been snatched out of my snatch...

Orally stimulate me, and
I don't just mean verbally, but
part my lips while placing
your skillful lips on my slit and
lick me ecstatically like you were
tasting my very soul, in fact,
suck on my clit until my soul
has been snatched out of
my snatch and what is left
of me is just a glistening shell,
abandoned on the beach of many.

"Feast on a Beach"
Zoetic Fyre

"Throbbing hearts, unruly palms, tongues flicking in and out, in a pool of intoxicating wet..."

A sea of people, all business-like, guzzling beer and wine,
Sat immersed in frisky small talk, even as your eyes sought the flame in mine.
Ravenous, pulsating, watchful, yet covert,
You toed the line, trying to fight the good fight.
What use, though, is your self-restraint now,
When you succumbed to the illicitness of us last night?

Throbbing hearts, unruly palms, tongues flicking in and out, in a pool of intoxicating wet,
Drunk silly as we were, this indiscretion is too tempting to forget.

Daytime's here, as we meet in the sun's glare,
Casting a veil on the dirty little secret we share.
You act indifferent, like nothing ever happened,
A bundle of contradictions—you walk dazed around me even as your pulse quickens.
Honey, why turn away from the blazing heat in my breasts?
When I can see your bulge down there,
Your nonchalance dissipating into sweat.
We can still talk transactions, billable hours and law firm targets,
But let's not stop being criminals stirring up the hornet's nest.

Do you not dream of dribbling on my juicy lips
    hidden
Behind a sheath of lace?
Or my twin babies (oops, boobies!) peeking at you
    from
Where the neckline meets the cleavage?

What stops you then from relishing me, raw and
    unfiltered, in my nakedness?
Is it the age gap, my marital status, or the boss label
    hanging on my blazer?
Please confess.

But speak your truth, undressed, bathed, and oiled,
As you pin my arms down on the bed, creasing the
    silk sheets,
Run me down like a dainty rag doll,
Show no mercy,
Play my jealous, jilted paramour
In the honeymoon suite.
Bite my lips, my neck, my nipples,
Bruise me red, bruise me blue,
Slip hard and rough between my thighs, into the
    Grand Canyon,
Show me who's the boss between us two.

"Happy Hour"
IRF

"Let me lose myself,

In the number of hands reaching for a piece of me..."

Slap me across my face.
Then choke me.
Shove my face to your dick,
So it can engulf me.
Disrespect me, so I question our future;
Right before you let your home boy grab my hair and
　　　throw me
To the bed, to catch me
Setting of this desecration,
Of my virginity,
To a 3 some forced;
Oops, I mean 4,
Maybe 5...
Let me drown in your lust.
Arms pulled back
In supplication,
Begging
For the gift of your body untethered.

Let all the days of your masculinity being questioned
Rain down vengeance on me!
Let me lose sight;
Except for your drilled in visions,
And his face thrusting epiphanies,
And his breast grabbing tendencies,
And his butt hole fantasies,
And his female insecurities,
That equate to rage against me.
That reverberates to my core,
Releasing a waterfall
Of ecstasy.
Bring all this aggression against me.
Let me lose myself,
In the number of hands reaching for a piece of me,
Releasing me from societal taboos
Of expectancy,
Of me being a *lady*.
When all I want is to be a play toy appreciated;

That's my fantasy.

"A Fantasy"
nora oz

"Wet drippings between the division
Of Her lower appendages
Is a signal of acceptance for my dimension"

I constrict
Around Her neck
To restrict
Her breathing
Just a bit
As she requested
And consented
Enough to make Her
Forbidden-fruit-pigmented lips
Open frequent
In an attempt
To breath-in sufficient
But the restriction
From my constriction
Has convinced
Her body to react when
My grip tightens
Breaths deepen
And Her reaction
Becomes a contradiction
She finds tranquility in my hand's tension
Encircling around Her esophagus
Providing pleasure by way of pressure
An Asphyxiated addiction

Complimenting Her prescription
From my seducing serpent
Slithering near Her midsection
With prey, being internal sensations
Sex is the affection
Affixed to Her attention
A kiss given without apprehension
To convert Her to my religion
Hands praising smoothly
Seducing moving inflictions
From two bodies in friction
Wordless descriptions
Of intimate sessions and temptations
Between glistening sections
When cavern meets erection
No discretion or protection
Once she is in the coil of my jurisdiction
I listen to the inhale and exhalations
Barely escaping
As my dirty diction directs her decision
In a conversation determining how
Wet drippings between the divisions
Of Her lower appendages
Is a signal of acceptance for my dimension
And recognition of the direction of my destination
As I patiently slither
And enter the sliver of Her snake den.

"Serpent's Seduction"
tonii

"Lift my legs up and enter my walls."

And suddenly, it goes dark.
As I sit here,
I hear footsteps walking back and forth.
The smell of the Black Tie candle from Bath and
    Body Works
And Smoke Woods from Walmart,
I'm into this and I know you're feeling this.
You walk near me and smell my Aromatherapy
    Sensual scent.
Kiss my lips seductively and back away.
Making me want to grab you, but I can't.
I can't because your silk ties are wrapped around my
    hands and eyes.
I don't want to breathe the wrong way.
I don't want to kill this moment—
Because I've been thinking about this all day.
You mentioned how you wanted to have your way with
    me,
And now you get to play.
Kiss my neck while you trickle ice down my body.
I want to grab you so much but that's not part of the
    game.
Spread my legs open and while you kiss on my
    breasts,
Insert the ice cubes into my pussy,
Making it numb so when you take me to the bedroom,
You can have your way with me.
Walk me to the bedroom,
Cake is on the menu.
Tie my hands to the bed
And dive in while my water drips on your beard so
    crazy.

Hmmmm, right there,
You're devouring this dessert.
Got you losing your mind while you're in between my
    legs.
Got me screaming,
Oh shit,
Got damn,
Hell yesss!
Use a feather and tickle my nipples,
Sending my body through an orgasmic ride.
Lift my legs up and enter my walls.
Let's let out that deep sigh,
While you explore my walls.
Whisper to me,
I hope it's everything you ever wanted.
As I scream yessssss,
I realize I'm having sex with my number one fan.
While my nails peel back your flesh,
I can't stop,
I won't stop,
I can't stop;
God don't stop.
Release yourself into me and kiss me,
With each releasing stroke.
Untie my eyes and look at me.
Tell me you love me,
And I say it back.
This silk tie is everything;
You have my soul.
Daddy,
Untie me.
What do you want me to cook?

"Silk Tie"
LP '2020

"Your legs open to accept my hand
You moan, eyes closed, pussy expands"

My alarm goes off, my eyes still shut
Fuck, I don't want to get up
But...

My eyes open and you are there
Laying beside me as you stare
I pull the covers off
Your body's bare.

My hand extends to touch your smooth skin
Our fingers lock, our connection begins
One kiss is the key and you let me in.

Your legs open to accept my hand
You moan, eyes closed, pussy expands
And then...

Sheets gripped as breathing deepens
Feelings tingle, pussy leakin'
In and out repetitions

My dick is swole, ready to insert
I climb on top and take off my shirt
Oh, shit it's time for work...

"Work On Site: Part 1"
tonii

"I'm excavating your trench And laying down every inch of my conduit"

I clock into your labia
My hands do manual labor on your clit
I'm excavating your trench
And laying down every inch of my conduit

I'm bulldozing with my Caterpillar
Draining your juices, moving shit around like a
          tractor
I'm attracted, no breaks, no relaxin'
I got deadlines to meet

I lift you up like a crane
To reach a different elevation
Up against the wall,
I dig deep for your foundation

My backhoe is excavating
I'm breaking into new depths with my drill
Cherry picking
Fork lifting
Hoisting you up on my steel

I'm the laborer, site supervisor, and project manager
I'm the operator, carpenter, electrician, and material
    handler
I'm digging, I'm lifting, I'm paving, and building
I'm hoisting, scaffolding, loading, and drilling

I see you trying to run from my hard hat
But my sling is making your ass cum back
To back
To back
To back

Don't try to combat this feeling from me drilling
Just let me compact that ass, as my hands are
    gripping and feeling

I'm working in between two mounds
I'm almost done with this work underground
You are yelling
You are screaming
I'm backfilling now

I got a large load for you and it's not dirt
Fuck, I'm cumming...
Where's my shirt?
I need to get up
And take my ass to work.

"Work On Site: Part 2"
tonii

"...I put your fingers in my mouth so I can suck the cum off them shits"

Let's go for a ride
And you know I live in Brooklyn so we can only go
    one of two ways
The Jackie got more curves than me
We've been smoking and drinking
Plus I want to suck your dick while driving so I think
    we should take the Belt Parkway
We start at Canarsie Pier
We go late enough
So you can bend me over a bench and no one can see
    us
Then we'll ride by Gateway
I'll let your fingers play
In a blink we almost go by the Burger King on
    Rockaway
I cum just a little bit
So we stop so you can get a cold sip
And I put your fingers in my mouth so I can suck the
    cum off them shits
Then I say which way
Do we
Proceed
And you say sit back bitch and roll this weed
I roll my eyes but in my mind I smile

Because I secretly like when you talk to me mean
So I roll up and look for a lighter to spark this joint
    as I enjoy this scene
Looking out the window
I see the top of the Ferris wheel
Then smile devilishly as it begins to rain
Knowing everyone will be gone
So Coney Island just became our personal field of
    play
I grab the bottle and the weed, and you say grab the
    umbrella please
So we can angle it for privacy
And proceed more inconspicuously
We then walk to the beach
Presuming this would happen
But you barely even let me lay it
Before you're licking my clit
Now I'm watching the shoreline seeing how the ocean
    hits it
When we are interrupted by beach patrol saying we
    gotta go
So I pull down my sundress in a hurry
Gathered myself so we could scurry
Only to reach the car and notice
That I forgot my undies
On the beach
At the end of the Belt Parkway

"Belt Parkway"
Meka J. Woods

Prepare for this Dick
This dope is going through you
Your new addiction.

"**Haiku #3**"
The Gentleman from San Francisco

"He bent my back over and my juices welcomed him freely"

He was always a bad habit of mine
A poet mixed in with a musician, both complementing
 each other
This situation was bound to be atomic
There's something about the way he played his guitar
 that made my legs want to separate and wrap
 around his waist
My divine feminine wanted his divine masculine in
 every way possible
We exchanged looks as he worked the room and I
 knew I had his attention
Crossed legs and flirtatious remarks at the bar made
 it obvious to us that it was time to take this a
 bit further
The cab ride to the hotel felt like pre-game
Lips locking and hands exploring
My heart was beating so fast that it made its own
 melody
Once in the room, we were greeted by mirrors on the
 ceiling and the wall
We hit the shower first where I devoured him
The water ran down my face like heavy rain as I took
 this king-like figure into my mouth
My face was repeatedly pressing up against his pelvis
 as he pounded my head
The room steamed over as his essence dripped down
 my throat
Grateful for his nectar as a response to my efforts, I
 smiled as I arose from my knees
Unafraid, he kissed me so passionately, I became
 lightheaded

He bent my back over and my juices welcomed him freely
Slippery when wet is such an understatement so we switched locations
We were wrestling on the bed until I was interrupted by a reflection over my head,
His body on top of mine and my legs resting on his shoulders
I'm best known for leading bedroom rebellions, so I fucked back proudly
He couldn't take my tightness yet, was still fucking like a stallion,
My body hung halfway off the bed as he was winning with every stroke and I didn't mind
He even had the audacity to spank me from behind just how I liked it
Whether I was looking at the wall or the ceiling I could see everything, and it was glorious
Refocusing my eyes back on my lover, I wanted to stay in the moment and enjoy every bit of it
Switching positions, my ass was spread wide on top of him as I glided up and down with ease
No coconut oil needed with the way I was creaming
He admired how good my ass looked on the ceiling, so I gave him a show
This wasn't my first rodeo, so I saddled up and dug my nails into his chest as I bounced my ass and he held on tight
By the end of the night, we both agreed that this was a much-needed workout
We went our separate ways and my legs were still humming well into 5 a.m. as I beat the sun home

"Mirrored Memories"
L. Rose

"I spotted Orion's belt while my pussy was eaten off the balcony."

It started in the Poconos,
The champagne tub with the pool in the room.
My legs straddled you and
We made love in the pool.
That was the first time you told me you loved me,
And made love to my pussy with your mouth.
We instantly began making love by the poolside.
Later,
We took our talents and ended up in Miami.
Fontainebleau was home for us.
We walked along the beach at night.
Heard the sounds of the ocean,
Glanced at the serene views of stars and the moon.
We had no choice but to fuck on top of the beach
       chairs.
I climaxed to such a sweet melody.
Later on,
Adult themed suite rooms began to enter our world.
Fuck me in the treehouse until I pass out,

Then wake up to more backshots.
Or take me in the ice cave,
And let's dance while we are making love.
Traveling the country and world with you is endless,
I want to explore more.
Take me back to DR Papi,
To Santiago and Puerto Plata.
In Santiago,
You fucked me on the roof and in the pool.
The view of the moon and stars was something I can't explain.
I spotted Orion's belt while my pussy was eaten off the balcony.
Puerto Plata took us to new heights,
As we
Learned to cum at the same time.
Releasing endorphins I never knew about.
Releasing fireworks like the Fourth of July.
Releasing a new energy.
Chemistry in our 30's.
Travel with me some more
So we can continue to explore.

"Oh, The Many Places We'll Fuck!"
LP'2020

"Flip me, lift me; I don't care

Just plunge already into my sweet

lair"

Do you trust me, you said, as the silk ribbon covered
    my eyes
How should I answer that when the darkness gave me
    a surprise?
For I have been told that nothing comes good from
    the dark
Excited, you observed
I think not, I tried to argue

As I don't know what will happen
Nor have I control over what will happen over me.
Obey me, you whispered in my ear
That is when your dark velvet voice unleashed its
    strings, and now I am your marionette
The next thing I know you were breathing fire on my
    skin
And that I can't stop myself from screaming
Toss and turn I go
But I can't seem to escape from your delicious torture
Flip me, lift me; I don't care
Just plunge already into my sweet lair

"Tie a Silky Ribbon"
Agni Locke

Your sensual growl
Lets me know you're ready
Now cum for Daddy

"Haiku #4"
The Gentleman from San Francisco

"His veins will pop out and I'll know he's ready."

I want you
I want you in a way that's not easily acceptable in
    today's society.
Let me tell you a story,
A story where I'm imagining every way I will touch
    you.
Let me begin with taking your shoes off,
Followed by your outside clothes.
I'll kiss your skin gently because you are perfect in
    every way.
Let me take off your wife beater and admire your
    tattoos.
I'll rub the details of them while playing with your
    chest hairs.
Next will be your golden trophy.
Let me take off your pants
And admire what you were blessed with.
I'll massage them gently with my hands and will add
    a little roughness with my mouth.
Let me suck you dry.

Deep throating every suck,
And when reaching the tip,
Suck hard and slow.
I'll treat it like a Blow Pop baby,
So you know what this mouth will do.
Let me teabag you.
And then put your testicles in my mouth.
I watch you while your eyes roll back.
And I'll feel my kitty-kat get wet for you.
Let me suck you one more time
And when he's at his peak,
His veins will pop out and I'll know he's ready.
I'll then straddle you with this juicy pussy.
Spread my cheeks and grab them tight
While my walls close in around your dick.
Pull me closer to you while I ride it nice and slow.
Later,
Choke me Papi while I bounce up and down.
Your dick will be my rodeo.
And I'm going to finish in first place.
But before you release,
I'll get off so you can cum on my face.

"I Want You"
LP'2020

Eyes become artists
Painting scenarios on
Your body's canvas

"Haiku #5"
The Gentleman from San Francisco

"My body;

Feels like ecstasy."

I could make you cum
Just by licking my cute, pink lips
And telling you I want some.

I could go down,
Massage the tip,
As I lick, lick, lick.

You see,
My body;
Feels like ecstasy.

I can ride you in reverse,
Make you think that a body this perfect has to be
      cursed.
Then call it simple foreplay.

I can bounce and make it clap,
Or go down on you and treat it like a snack.

My favorite thing to do for you is strip.
Slowly drop the red lace,
Before I ride your face.

I can tease you,
By telling you *I just want to please you.*

I can beg you to cum.
And tell you I want to taste some.

My mouth's on the tip,
As my hands rub the shaft,
I'm giving little work but it's making you react.
And then I'll whisper gently in your ear, *Baby, hit it
    from the back.*

"Temptations"
B.S.

"Imperceptive but I feel the sight of Her face filled with my appendage"

My eyes open to darkness in every direction
My hands cuffed behind my back to a chair
My body bare, stripped of every piece of clothing
Perplexed, I blindly cry out, "Is anyone there?"

My voice echoes in space, my ears anxiously seeks sound
My heart rate increasing, as "nothing" is what I hear
My breathing now deepening I wiggle a little where I sit
I'm nervous but anxious with questions of what, why and where

Then, I hear a door open and shut softly and a familiar sound begins
The rhythm of 4" high stiletto heels pacing gracefully coming near
Each step aligns with each one of my breaths taken in and out
I cease resisting my restraints and nervously asks, "Who is here?"

The last step ends on the right side of where I sit,
    cuffed and naked
Then, my nose detects a well-known scent, the one
    "she" seldomly wears
That fragrance summons recollections of our sex
    sessions
Constructing the grin on my face as she whispers in
    my ear

"Are you ready for this pussy?" she says, blunt and
    intimately with more tongue in Her diction
I, being stunned, stutter, as a staggered "yes" from
    my lips appear
Deep breaths while erection develops with each step
    of those heels
I, then, become braille for Her hands as she reads me
    in this chair

My shoulders read squeeze me, my neck reads choke
    me
My chest she reads slowly, and my abdomen is
    where...
Her hands lead down to bent knees, reading my thighs
    as they open
She then reads my erection like a verse, a scripture,
    or a prayer

Imperceptive but I feel the sight of Her face filled
    with my appendage
Oral dictation, stimulation in the words that she
    shares
Translations of my non-verbal communication, my
    body is a demonstration
Of the transformation from physically visual into
    sexual oration

After stiff, rigid, firm, and hardened in Her jaws
She now perches Her nude physique on my lap, and
    inside of Her snare
Her rise and fall, Her tidal motions are constant
I melt to become a wave that she surfs in midair

She lays back, Her hips rotate and shifts
With Her head back she grabs my head in this blinded
    affair
Long stroking every inch as I am forced to concede
Then, shiver, shake, cease, and tremble, all while
    gripping my hair

Her orgasm, sporadic but intense and passionate
Astonished, euphoric, paralysis, she sits still like a stare
She slowly stands to Her feet and extracts me from within Her depths
"Thank you" she whispers, heels stride as they came, silent again, she disappeared

I wonder if this was real or was it just a dream that I had
Being blindfolded and dominated, while handcuffed to a chair
Without my vision, no witness or proof
But I love the idea of being fucked by a woman who was never there.

"Blinded"
tonii

"Performing fellatio until my tonsils go numb and your toes curl..."

You had that thing that I wanted so bad
I mean, I had it but I didn't at the same time
Our vibe was always a bit weird sometimes
Either way, you had that thing and I wanted it
You're a pure cacao chocolate brown skin brotha with
    a smile that always took my breath away
I wanted you in the worst ways possible, my blues and
    my funk in both thighs
I knew what time it was whenever you'd give me that
    certain look
I reminisce on the days back when you use to tap jazz
    beats on my thigh as we sat in traffic
I remember wishing that your hand would explore a
    bit further and touch my womanly nature
Late night drives became our favorite pastime
We'd park near a body of water and my body would
    immediately overflow with desires
I wanted to play surfboard in the backseat as we
    steamed up the windows, heating the vehicle
    without the need for the heater to be on

Hugging,
Touching,
Kissing,
Rubbing,
Licking and sucking,
I wanted to make your body lose all control
Mighty lion king, this lioness wanted to put your pride at ease
Exceeding your every expectation,
Performing fellatio until my tonsils go numb and your toes curl as you have an outer body experience
I never wasted a drop of your sweet nectar and this fantasy is no different
Hold on tight to my body as we work up a sweat moving up and down creating a rhythm, turning my waistline into a bassline as I rock and squeeze into ecstasy
We'd make the car seem like a party bus with our noise making and the car moving
You'd feel intoxicated and my legs would feel like gelatin by the time we finish
The next best thing would be cuddling while listening to the rain, nothing else would matter at that moment…

"Backseat Fantasies"
L. Rose

"we adding to the saxophonic symphony with my cacophonous moans."

Hun?
Let's take a
slow ride down I-95.
We'll start here, near
the top in New York City
where our lips will meet,
then we will descend
down the highway
nibbling on necks
as we travel along the path.
We'll get carried away
fondling endless loops while
detouring through Maryland's 295.
After some time and
handsy attention
we'll eventually circle back to
our proper route
with
tongues
slowly
licking
their way
down south
enjoying views along
side roads and
pausing
to take a splash
in the navel town of Bath, North Carolina

before my head goes down
to the tip of Florida.
I want to enjoy the entirety
of this peninsula state
taking it all in,
in hands on ways and
tasting all
the local flavors
and savoring
the moment.
But before this road trip is done
make sure you
take a long swimming dip
in to my gulf city,
Sweetie.
In fact,
Baby, maybe
we can just
move there together
making it our permanent
state of being,
we adding to the saxophonic
symphony with my
cacophonous moans.
Or maybe Love,
we stay nowhere
and just travel everywhere
that this pleasure can take us to
with no boundaries or borders
during this trip as we seek our bliss.
Honey, this car is ready,
let's go for that ride down 95.

"I-95 Ride"
Zoetic Fyre

"...getting sloppy while the tip of your dick is touching my tonsils"

Let me take you to a place where you can escape
Let's keep it on a need to know basis
As I twist my hips and lick my lips while you make all kinds of faces
Admitting that you can't take it, I won't stop until you climax
Gripping your shaft as you fantasize about slapping my ass while I throw it back or getting sloppy while the tip of your dick is touching my tonsils
I want your intellectual to overload as I make your body orgasm and your mind explode thinking about my words penetrating the depths of your inner sapiosexual
I'm here to make your waters overflow
You will taste my juices on the tip of your tongue as my words creep from your mind, licking and sucking every inch of your body

Every time your knees buckle you will think of me,
    satisfying your every want and need
And just like a fiend, you will be jonesing for me
My words will have you think about my honey
    dripping on your lips at random times of the
    day,
Flashing back to the night before when you thought of
    my pussy making a gushing noise as I go up
    and down on your dick, gripping the base of
    your shaft and letting go once I've reached the
    tip
Creaming as I rock my hips and dig my nails into
    your chest
You will think of me as some kind of priestess with
    that good juju between my legs
But really, I'm just a master wordsmith letting all
    these metaphors and similes roll off my tongue
    as you peak
Or maybe I am both
Either way, I aim to please
You're welcome...

"Seduction of the Mind"
L. Rose

"Concentrated penetration
Penetrated your concentration"

I don't know where I placed my mind
But it's gone like the sun that does not shine
Or clocks that don't share time
Or my 2 eyes both gone blind
See...
I'm missing the curve in your spine
When the sheets meet your face
With your ass up
I embrace you from behind
Regulate your snake like motions

Skin to skin rhythm
Clean stroking within your dirty wine
Put a collar on your pussy cat
To make Her mine
Sheets soaking
Deep throat
Being one of your favorite past times
Concentrated penetration
Penetrated your concentration
Dick head misplaced inside
In other words,
The reason it's so hard to find
Is because your pussy makes me
Lose my mind.

"Lose My Mind"
tonii

"I beg and plead for him to touch me one more time."

I can feel his fingers brushing over my lips.
As moisture collects between my thighs,
I beg and plead for him to touch me one more time.

I can feel his lips against my ear,
"You mean like this?"
As he brushes his fingers against my clit.

My mind is going haywire with desire.

I can feel my moans send him into a state where he
    bites his juicy lip.
All I can think, in this moment, is how much I want a
    taste of his juicy dick.
Even just one little lick.

I can feel the kisses as he moves up my leg,
As he slows his kissing,
I can tell he's playing a game.

For a moment in time,
I feel alone in the darkness.

Awaiting what's next,
I feel his mouth against my breast.
He kisses and licks as his fingers find my soaking hole.

I can't help but to let out a huge moan.

He pushes me back so I'm laying against the bed.
He then proceeds to give me head.

Moan after moan,
I feel it getting closer.
The moment where the universe freezes as I cream the sheets.

Then it happens,
The darkness I've been seeing feels so light.
As my legs begin to tense up and feel tight.

I feel the blindfold getting pulled away from my eyes.
He gives me a kiss and whispers,
"Baby, you're all mine."

"Darkness"
B.S.

"...my words are inside of you, The creation of Legible penetration"

My words are now in your mind
Each line of my poem
Forms imagery of what I want you to feel and see
You read, "I am licking the gush out of your pussy
And the sound of mushy mac and cheese
Surrounds me in what I am doing"
And immediately you envision me between thighs
With your two eyes focused on me
While my tongue exposes clitoris
Your insides now open and moist accumulation drips
Creating bliss inside of your panties
Until they are soaking
In natural lubrication
...
Be advised
These are just words that you are reading
But after reaching your mind
You find my words transforming into your fantasies
Believing that you are in control
You keep reading

Then, you reach the next line
"My 9-inch curved banana dick is now swole
And I am ready to deposit it
Into the slit in your cockpit
So your pussy can swallow it whole"
You gasp
As you are imagining my shaft disappearing
Inside of your lips as they clasp onto it
You want to stop
But you've read to much into this
Now my description of this erection
Has implanted a vivid image of my curved appendage
Being placed in your face for examination
I hear your breathing
With one hand on your waist
And the other squeezing your breast
I feel your heart beating, increasing its pace
And your eyes try to close
But can't because your body now knows
And mouth waters for a taste
And the only way to draw closer is to
...
Keep reading
...

So I elaborate
"My hands slide up your skirt
And my fingers walk along your inner thighs
As you bite your lips, with your head back
I hear soft tones of moans and silent cries
I latch onto to your panties
And guide them to your feet
Your chest rise, back arched
You now slightly tremble in your seat"
(Inhale)
(Exhale)
Breathe
Because breaths are needed
After my words become a fetish that you are reading
You cross your legs in an attempt to cease the
     sensations
But my words are inside of you,
The creation of
Legible penetration
And each line is a stroke
Intended for intensification
My words impregnating your mind
With intense poetic ejaculation
...

"I'm deep within
I pull out and then
I thrust back again
Pull out and then
Push in again
Repeat times 10
Then, I release my kin
Jerk, shake, and tremble happens
You now glisten
On the outside and within"
...
I came into your head
By way of words
In the lines of poetry
That you have now read.

"Read Me"
tonii

INDEX

Desire in Poem Form - Zoetic Fyre	2
Blindfolded Sex - DP	6
Dark and Twisted - The Black Rose	8
Warhol - tonii	10
Round One - The Gentleman from San Francisco	12
Saran Wrap and Bandanas - Zoetic Fyre	14
Haiku #4 - The Gentleman from San Francisco	17
Cave's Sweet Torture - Agni Locke	18
A Birthday Gift - IRF	20
Questions - nora oz	26
Happy Birthday Darling - The Black Rose	28
Memoirs of Our Labias - LP'2020, nora oz, & Zoetic Fyre	30
The Threesome I Always Coveted - DP	36
Surprise - The Gentleman from San Francisco	38
Blindfolded - Meka J. Woods	42
Loving in Five Haikus - Zoetic Fyre	45
Slurp Fest - IRF	46
Haikus of Stimulation - The Black Rose	51
A Night to Remember - L. Rose	52
Wake Me Up - DP	54
Sighkus - nora oz	57
More - LP'2020	58
The God Spot - B.S.	60
Haiku #5 - The Gentleman from San Francisco	63
In My House - DP	64
I Will Not Think of England - Agni Locke	66
Passport - The Black Rose	68
Salad Bar - Meka J. Woods	70
Orate - tonii	72
Feast on a Beach - Zoetic Fyre	75
Happy Hour - IRF	76
A Fantasy - nora oz	78
Serpent's Seduction - tonii	80
Silk Tie - LP'2020	82
Work On Site: Part 1 - tonii	85
Work On Site: Part 2 - tonii	86
Belt Parkway - Meka J. Woods	88
Haiku #1 - The Gentleman from San Francisco	91
Mirrored Memories - L. Rose	92
Oh, The Many Places We'll Fuck! - LP'2020	94
Tie a Silky Ribbon - Agni Locke	96
Haiku #3 - The Gentleman from San Francisco	99
I Want You - LP'2020	100
Haiku #2 - The Gentleman from San Francisco	103
Temptations - B.S.	104
Blinded - tonii	106
Backseat Fantasies - L. Rose	110
I-95 Ride - Zoetic Fyre	112
Seduction of the Mind - L. Rose	114
Lose My Mind - tonii	116
Darkness. - B.S.	118
Read Me - tonii	120

*"Erotic poetry awakens the sleeping spirit of pleasure
And unifies us in a universal human trait
...
Desire."*

-tonii

Came.

www.ingramcontent.com/pod-product-compliance
Lightning Source LLC
Chambersburg PA
CBHW070915080526
44589CB00013B/1297